Understanding the

# ELECTORAL COLLEGE

WHAT'S UP with Your Government?

Alicia Klepeis

PowerKiDS press
New York

Published in 2018 by **The Rosen Publishing Group, Inc.**
29 East 21st Street, New York, NY 10010

Cataloging-in-Publication Data
Names: Klepeis, Alicia Z..
Title: Understanding the electoral college / Alicia Z. Klepeis.
Description: New York : PowerKids Press, 2018. | Series: What's up with your government? | Includes index.
Identifiers: LCCN ISBN 9781538323243 (pbk.) | ISBN 9781538322284 (library bound) | ISBN 9781538323250 (6 pack)
Subjects: LCSH: Electoral college--United States--Juvenile literature. | Presidents--United States--Election--Juvenile literature.
Classification: LCC JK529.K55 2018 | DDC 324.6'3--dc23



First Edition

Developed and Produced by Focus Strategic Communications, Inc.
Project Manager: Adrianna Edwards
Editor: Ron Edwards
Design and Composition: Ruth Dwight
Copyeditors: Adrianna Edwards, Francine Geraci
Media Researchers: Adrianna Edwards, Paula Joiner
Proofreader: Francine Geraci
Index: Ron Edwards, Maddi Nixon

Photo Credits: Credit Abbreviations: NARA National Archives and Records Administration; S Shutterstock.Position on the page: T: top, B: Bottom, C: Center, L: left, R: right. Cover TL: Frontpage/S, TR: Niyazz/S, CL: Carsten Reisinger/S, B: DNetromphotos/S; 1 TL: Frontpage/S, TR: Niyazz/S, CL: Carsten Reisinger/S; 4: Gino Santa Maria/S; 5: Burlingham/S; 6: Rawpixel.com/S; 7: txking/S; 8: DNetromphotos/S; 9: vepar5/S; 11: Architect of the Capitol; 12: Everett Historical/S; 13: Billion Photos/S; 14, 15: Everett Historical/S; 16: U.S. Department of the Interior | U.S. Geological Survey; 17: Bakhtiar Zein/S; 18, 19: Gregory Reed/S; 20: Barbara Kalbfleisch/S; 21 T: TeddyandMia/S, B: Susan Schmitz/S; 22: Joseph Sohm/S; 23: Robert Biedermann/S; 24: Volina/S; 25: NARA; 26: Valiik/S; 27 L: stocklight/S, R: Joseph Sohm/S; 29 TL: Everett Historical/S, BR: Rena Schild/S; Design Elements: Nella/S, tassita numsri/S.



Manufactured in the United States of America

CPSIA Compliance Information: Batch BW18PK: For Further Information contact Rosen Publishing, New York, New York at 1-800-237-9932.

# CONTENTS


Ready, Set, Vote! .......................... 4

The Electoral College Develops .......................... 10

All About Electors .......................... 16

Election Day to Inauguration Day .......................... 20

Future of the Electoral College .......................... 26

Glossary .......................... 30

Further Information .......................... 31

Index .......................... 32

# READY, SET, VOTE!

## THE 2016 PRESIDENTIAL ELECTION

On November 8, 2016, American voters went to the **polls** across the country. More than 128 million people voted in this general election. Most people thought they were voting to choose the next president and vice president of the United States. But in fact, voters were choosing members of the Electoral College. What is the Electoral College? Read on to find out!

Donald Trump, shown here on March 11, 2016 during his election campaign, went on to be the 45th president of the United States.

# Presidential Elections in the United States

U.S. elections for president and vice president are held every four years. The date may vary from one election to the next. But ever since Congress passed a federal law in 1845, they are always held on the Tuesday after the first Monday in November.

Voting is not required by law in the United States, unlike some countries. U.S. citizens aged 18 and older are eligible to vote, but they can choose whether they do so or not.

## FAST FACT

Some countries hold their presidential elections on the weekends to make it easier for people to get to the polls.

# WHAT IS THE ELECTORAL COLLEGE?

The Electoral College is not somewhere young adults go to school. In fact, it's not a place at all. It is actually a process. The word "college" just refers to an organized group of people who are engaged in a shared task. What is the Electoral College's task? To elect a president and vice president for our country.

The people who are part of the Electoral College are called **electors**. Electors are chosen by political parties. States have different processes for choosing electors.

Electors are a very diverse group of people. They come from all walks of life.

## COLLEGE ELECTORS

The Electoral College has 538 members. This number might seem random, but there is a reason for it.

This total is equal to the number of members of the House of Representatives (435) plus the number of senators in the U.S. Senate (100) plus three members from the District of Columbia.

Although Hillary Clinton won the **popular vote**, Donald Trump won the electoral vote. This poll shows Trump in the lead for electoral votes.

**538 =** the number of representatives in the U.S. House of Representatives (435)
+ the number of senators in the U.S. Senate (100)
+ members from the District of Columbia (3)

## FAST FACT

Washington, DC, which is not an actual state, has no representatives in Congress. But as the capital of the country, it does have three electoral votes.

# ELECTORS BY STATE

Have you ever seen a TV broadcast on election night? If so, you probably noticed one very important map. It's the map of Electoral College votes. There are 538 electoral votes for the whole country. States that vote for the Republican Party show up as red. States that vote for the Democrats show up as blue.

Every state has a certain number of electoral votes. How is that number decided? The number of electoral votes each state receives equals its number of members in the U.S. House of Representatives plus its two senators. Every state, regardless of its size, gets two senators, while the number of representatives is based on a state's population.

California is the state with the biggest population, so it also has the largest number of electoral votes—55. Texas has 38 votes. New York and Florida each have 29 votes. Some low-population states, such as Alaska, have only three electoral votes.

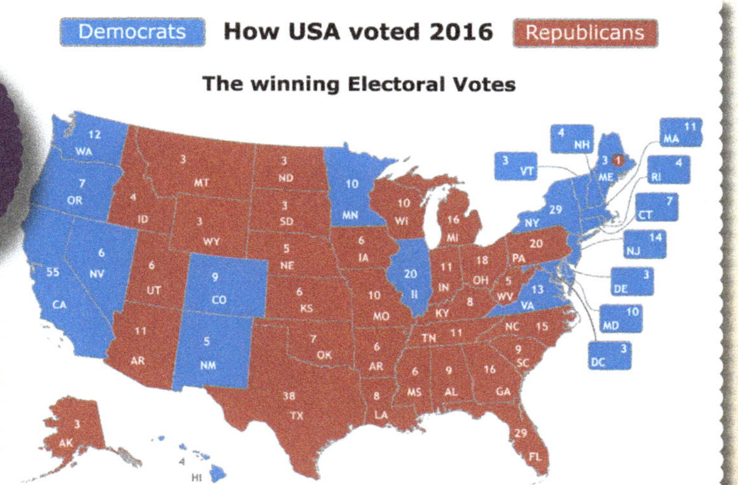


This map shows the results of the U.S. presidential election on November 8, 2016.

# Do All Votes Count the Same?

Across the United States, people go to vote at the polls. Every person's vote counts equally within a state. It's definitely important to vote. But there is no doubt that bigger states have a bigger impact in the Electoral College. While California has 55 electoral votes, South Dakota has only three. Since it takes 270 electoral votes to win the presidency, California has much more sway in electing a president than South Dakota does.

Often, but not always, states with the largest number of electoral votes, such as California, decide the winner of the election.

## FAST FACT

There are seven states with just three electoral votes: Alaska, Idaho, Montana, North Dakota, South Dakota, Vermont, and Wyoming.

# THE ELECTORAL COLLEGE DEVELOPS

## WHY DO WE HAVE AN ELECTORAL COLLEGE?

Why does the U.S. have an Electoral College? The answer goes way back—to our nation's Founding Fathers.

In 1787, **delegates** from all states except Rhode Island met in Philadelphia. These delegates were working to strengthen our country's national government. The **Framers** of the Constitution felt average citizens shouldn't have the power to directly elect the president. They believed most people were not well-informed enough to make such a big decision. Remember that 230 years ago, people didn't learn about candidates through television, radio, or the Internet. Even newspapers back then were slow to distribute information.

### FAST FACT

**The United States is the only country in the world that elects its president and vice president with an Electoral College.**

★ ★ ★ ★ ★ ★ ★ ★ ★ ★ ★ ★ ★ ★ ★ ★ ★ ★ ★ ★ ★

### HOW THE ELECTORAL COLLEGE WAS FORMED

The Framers also worried that people would just support candidates from their own states. Some thought the presidents would only come from states with big populations. In the end, the Founding Fathers made a decision. U.S. citizens would elect electors. In turn, the electors would choose the best candidate to become president. At this time, women didn't have the right to vote or run for president.

## Other Suggestions on How to Elect a President

At the 1787 Constitutional Convention in Philadelphia, various people suggested at least four ways to elect the president and vice president. One was election by Congress. Another was election by state governors. A third was election by state legislatures. There was also the suggestion of direct election by voters.

The Founding Fathers signed the U.S. Constitution at the Constitutional Convention in Philadelphia in 1787. This 20- by 30-foot (6 by 9 m) painting hangs prominently in the U.S. Capitol.

# EARLY PROBLEMS WITH THE ELECTORAL COLLEGE

When the Founding Fathers came up with their system of the Electoral College, they thought the electors should be allowed to vote however they wanted. The person who received the most votes from the electors would become president. The person with the next highest number of votes would become vice president. But this system didn't last long. Why not?

In 1800, two candidates each received the same number of votes from the electors. (They were Thomas Jefferson and Aaron Burr.) The Constitution said the House of Representatives had to break the tie. It took 36 **ballots** to break the tie. Jefferson finally won with a **majority** of votes.

Thomas Jefferson

Aaron Burr

## AMENDMENT XII

After the 1800 election, the electoral system changed. The Twelfth **Amendment** to the Constitution was **ratified** in 1804. It made the electoral procedure clearer. It said that each elector would vote for one person for president and another person for vice president. This system is still in place today.

The Twelfth Amendment of the U.S. Constitution described how the electors' voting process would work.

### FAST FACT

Electors cannot vote for a presidential and vice presidential candidate who both come from their own home state.

# OTHER CONTROVERSIES AND UNUSUAL ELECTIONS

Over its history, the Electoral College experienced a number of unusual circumstances. The 1800 Jefferson–Burr tie vote was not the only unusual experience for the Electoral College.

In 1824, Andrew Jackson won more electoral votes than the other top three contenders. (They were John Quincy Adams, William Crawford, and Henry Clay.) But none of these candidates had a majority of electoral votes. A majority is needed to win the presidency. What happened? The House of Representatives chose Adams, even though Jackson won more of the popular vote.

Andrew Jackson lost even though he had more votes.

John Quincy Adams became the sixth president of the United States following the controversial election of 1824.

## THE ELECTION OF 1876

People often refer to the year 1876 as the "disputed" election. Democratic candidate Samuel J. Tilden beat Republican Rutherford B. Hayes in the popular vote. Tilden received 184 electoral votes, just one short of a clear majority.

There were 20 outstanding votes in dispute. Congress took action. It created a commission to review these disputed electoral votes. In the end, the commission awarded all of the disputed votes to Rutherford Hayes, making him the victor at 185 to 184! Days later, Hayes became the 19th U.S. president.

# The Vice President Chosen by the Senate

Only once in U.S. history did a vice presidential candidate not receive a majority of electoral votes. In 1836, Richard Mentor Johnson was the running mate of Martin Van Buren. He fell one vote short of the 148 electoral votes needed to become vice president. So what happened? The Twelfth Amendment was put to work. According to the amendment's terms, the Senate chose the vice president. Johnson became the ninth vice president.

The election of 1836 featured Richard M. Johnson (pictured here) and Martin Van Buren.

# ALL ABOUT ELECTORS

## WHO CAN BE AN ELECTOR?

In 1787, when the Electoral College was created, it had fewer electors than today. After all, there were fewer states at that time. And far fewer people lived in the United States. But since the Electoral College's earliest days, the number of electors has been based on the same formula. It's the number of representatives and senators from the 50 states plus three electors from the District of Columbia.

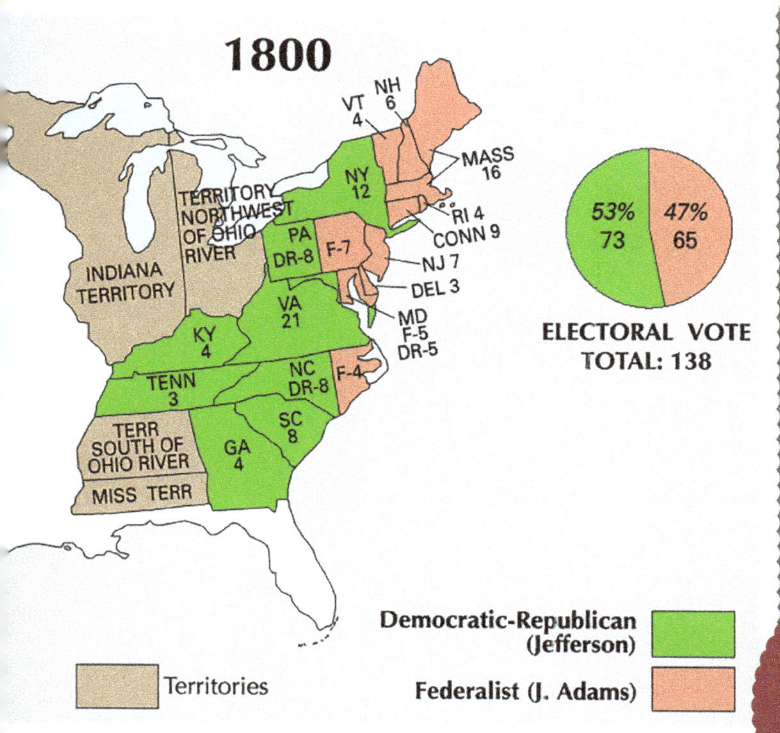


In 1787, there were only three confirmed states in the new union. By 1800, that number had grown to 16.

## LIMITS ON ELECTORS

The U.S. Constitution actually puts very few limits on who can be an elector. U.S. Senators cannot be electors. Neither can members of the U.S. House of Representatives. The U.S. Constitution also says that no person "holding an Office of Trust or Profit under the United States" can be appointed as an elector. This means that employees of the federal government cannot be electors.

There are very few restrictions on who can be chosen as an elector.

### FAST FACT

**The oldest known elector in the 2016 Electoral College was 93-year-old Hazel Ingram, whose grandmother was born into slavery. Ingram was chosen by the Working Families Party to be a New York State elector.**

## HOW ARE ELECTORS CHOSEN?

Choosing electors is a two-part process. To begin with, the political parties in each state choose lists of possible electors known as **slates** sometime before the general election. The process of choosing potential electors varies from state to state. A political party's central committee might **nominate** potential electors at their state party convention. This often happens in the summer, several months before the popular vote.

Electors are nominated at state party conventions.

## WHO GETS NOMINATED?

What types of people are nominated to be electors? People are often suggested if they have provided service to a particular political party. Sometimes people who have donated a lot of money to a political campaign are chosen. People who have a personal connection with the party's presidential candidate may also be selected as possible electors.

### Surprise Electors

During the 2016 general election, New York State had 29 electors. One of those was former President Bill Clinton. Others included prominent Democrats such as New York Governor Andrew Cuomo and New York City Mayor Bill de Blasio.

Bill Clinton served as one of the New York State electors in the 2016 election.

# ELECTION DAY TO INAUGURATION DAY

## WHAT ACTUALLY HAPPENS ON ELECTION DAY?

Part two of the elector-selecting process happens on Election Day in early November. This is when citizens of the United States cast their ballots to choose electors from their state.

It might seem as though people are voting for president and vice president at the polls. Many people are not aware that they do not vote directly for a president or vice president. They are actually voting for electors, who then get to elect the president and vice president.

On Election Day, signs such as this are often placed outside polling stations, such as schools.

**FAST FACT**

In 2004, there were over 100,000 polling stations in the United States.

## Election Date

Election Day is always in November, but it falls on different days. Officially, Election Day is "the Tuesday next after the first Monday in the month of November" or "the first Tuesday after November 1." In other words, the earliest it can occur is November 2, and the latest is November 8.

The 2016 election was held on November 8, the latest date that a presidential election can be held.

### WHO IS ON THE BALLOTS?

In many states the electors' names don't even appear on the ballots. Voters see only the presidential and vice presidential candidates' names on the ballots. But actually they are voting for the electors of a particular political party.

An early voting ballot form from the 2016 election shows the names of the presidential and vice presidential candidates as well as their parties' electors.

# POPULAR VOTES VERSUS ELECTORAL VOTES

People cast their votes on Election Day in voting booths across the nation. Depending on the state, people vote in various ways. Some vote on pieces of paper. Others vote on computer screens.

These votes are recorded. Each state and the District of Columbia tallies its votes. In 48 states, the (presidential) candidate who receives the most popular votes wins all of that state's electoral votes. It's a winner-takes-all system. The other two states, Maine and Nebraska, are a little different.

People cast their votes in booths similar to this in Ventura County, California.

## FAST FACT

During the 2000 election between George W. Bush and Al Gore, the voting results for Florida were very close. Bush was just 327 votes ahead of Gore following a recount. "Hanging chads" (paper ballots that were partially punched by voters) made finalizing the results very difficult.

## A CLOSER LOOK

Let's look at the 2016 election. Nearly 4 million people voted for Donald Trump in California. That's a lot of people. But Hillary Clinton had more of the popular vote. Over 7 million people voted for her. So she received all of California's electoral votes.

| Party | Candidate | Percentage | Actual Vote |
|---|---|---|---|
| Democrat | Hillary Clinton | 61.6% | 7,362,490 |
| Republican | Donald Trump | 32.8% | 3,916,209 |
| Others | All others | 5.6% | 675,618 |

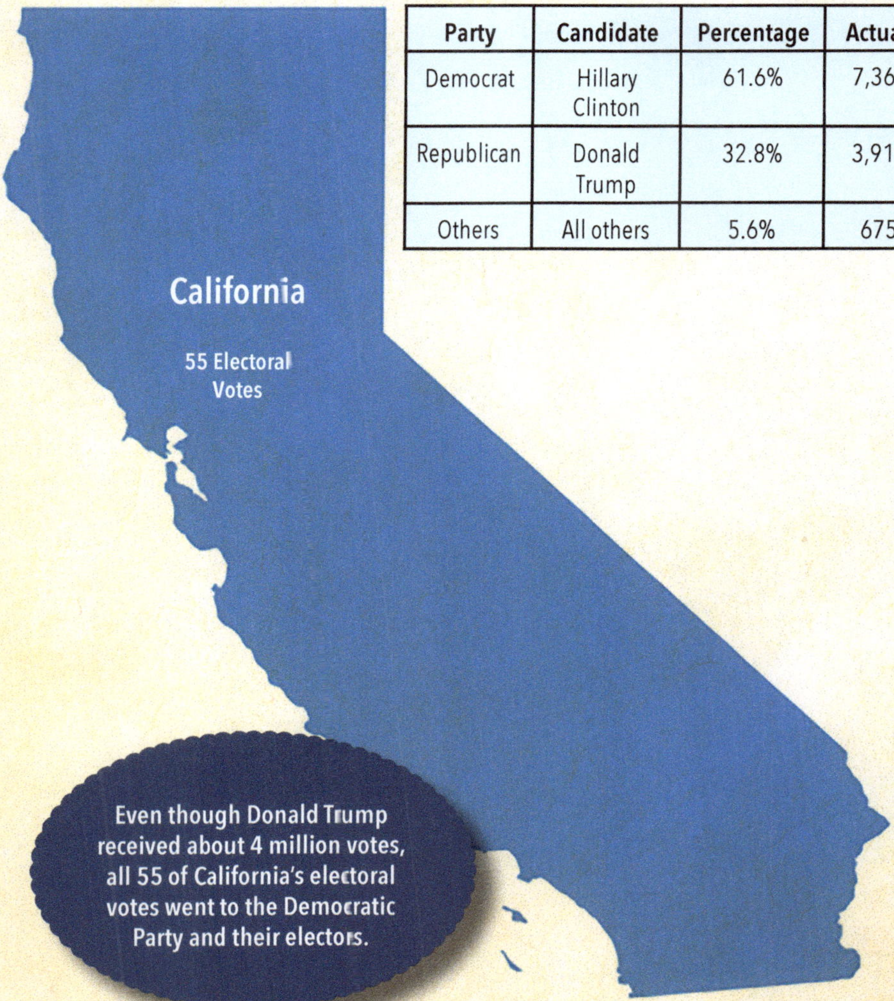


Even though Donald Trump received about 4 million votes, all 55 of California's electoral votes went to the Democratic Party and their electors.

# Nebraska and Maine — The Other Two States

Nebraska and Maine have a different system for how their electoral votes are determined. Instead of a winner-takes-all system, Maine and Nebraska can divide their electoral votes among different candidates.

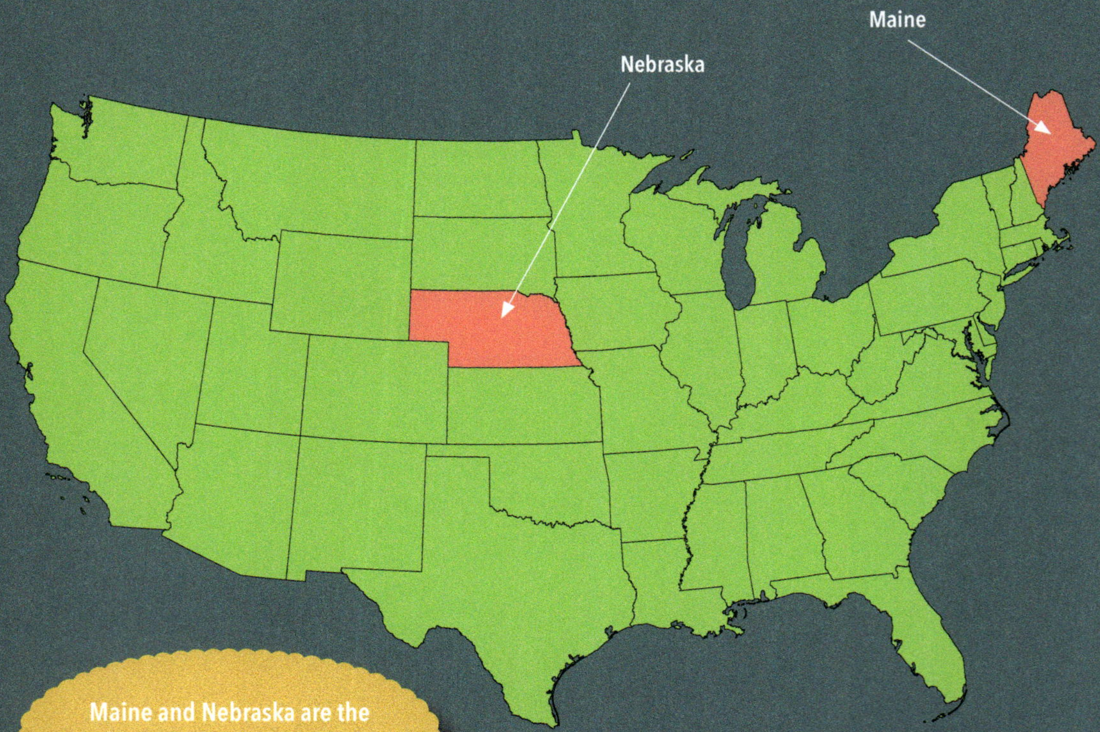


Maine and Nebraska are the only states that do not use the winner-takes-all system.

## FAST FACT

On January 20 of the year following the election, the president-elect takes the oath of office. They are sworn in as the president of the United States.

# THE ELECTORS MEET AND VOTE

Normally by the end of election night, the country knows who won. But the president is not *officially* elected yet. Following the general election, the members of the Electoral College meet in their respective state capitals to cast their votes for president and vice president. They do this in December, and those votes are recorded and sent to Congress.

Then, in January, each state's electoral votes are counted in a joint session of Congress. The official results are tallied, and the winning candidates who have been elected president and vice president of the United States are announced.

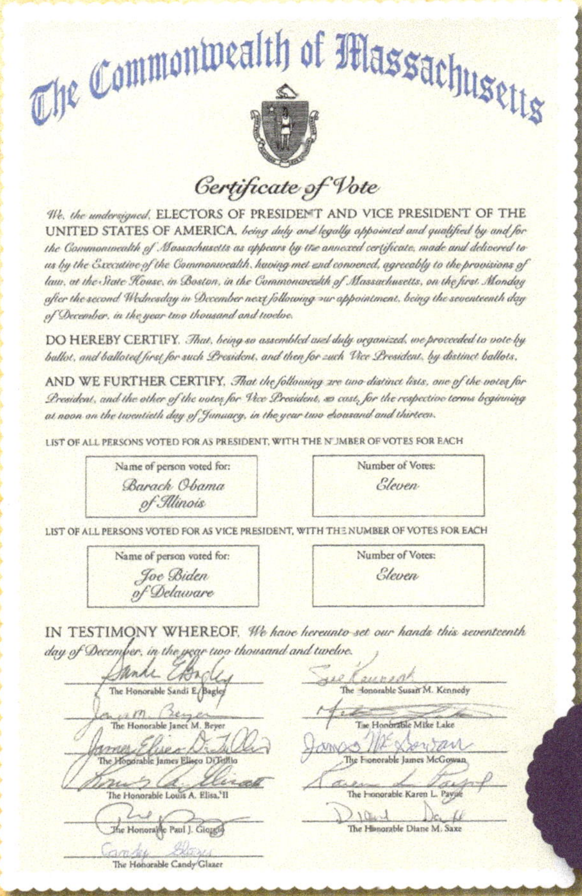

The Commonwealth of Massachusetts

Certificate of Vote

We, the undersigned, ELECTORS OF PRESIDENT AND VICE PRESIDENT OF THE UNITED STATES OF AMERICA, being duly and legally appointed and qualified by and for the Commonwealth of Massachusetts as appears by the annexed certificate, made and delivered to us by the Executive of the Commonwealth, having met and convened, agreeably to the provisions of law, at the State House, in Boston, in the Commonwealth of Massachusetts, on the first Monday after the second Wednesday in December next following our appointment, being the seventeenth day of December, in the year two thousand and twelve.

DO HEREBY CERTIFY, That, being so assembled and duly organized, we proceeded to vote by ballot, and balloted first for such President, and then for such Vice President, by distinct ballots.

AND WE FURTHER CERTIFY, That the following are two distinct lists, one of the votes for President, and the other of the votes for Vice President, so cast, for the respective terms beginning at noon on the twentieth day of January, in the year two thousand and thirteen.

LIST OF ALL PERSONS VOTED FOR AS PRESIDENT, WITH THE NUMBER OF VOTES FOR EACH

| Name of person voted for: | Number of Votes: |
|---|---|
| Barack Obama of Illinois | Eleven |

LIST OF ALL PERSONS VOTED FOR AS VICE PRESIDENT, WITH THE NUMBER OF VOTES FOR EACH

| Name of person voted for: | Number of Votes: |
|---|---|
| Joe Biden of Delaware | Eleven |

IN TESTIMONY WHEREOF, We have hereunto set our hands this seventeenth day of December, in the year two thousand and twelve.

The Honorable Sandi E. Bagley
The Honorable Susan M. Kennedy
The Honorable Janet M. Beyer
The Honorable Mike Lake
The Honorable James Eliseo DiTullio
The Honorable James McGowan
The Honorable Louis A. Elisa, II
The Honorable Karen L. Payne
The Honorable Paul J. Giorgio
The Honorable Diane M. Saxe
The Honorable Candy Glazer

Certificates of Vote, similar to this one from Massachusetts in 2012, are completed for each state and submitted to Congress.

# FUTURE OF THE ELECTORAL COLLEGE

## WHAT IF AN ELECTOR CHANGES THEIR MIND?

According to the Constitution, electors do not have to vote for a particular candidate. However, some states require electors to vote according to the popular vote in their states.

It is very unusual for an elector to vote against their party's pledged candidate. But it does happen now and again. Electors who break their pledge are often called "faithless electors."

Faithless electors are those who do not vote for their party's candidate.

## Faithless Electors in the 2016 Election

In 2016, seven electors voted for someone other than their party's nominee. Five were supposed to vote for Clinton. Two were supposed to vote for Trump. Instead these faithless electors voted for a variety of people. These included noncandidates Colin Powell, Bernie Sanders, and Faith Spotted Eagle (a Native American activist). That is the highest number of faithless electors in any U.S. presidential election.

Colin Powell

Bernie Sanders

### FAST FACT

Faithless electors may be fined or disqualified for breaking their pledge. But according to the National Archives, no elector has ever been **prosecuted** for not voting as pledged.

# THE ELECTORAL COLLEGE TODAY

Throughout U.S. history, people have questioned whether the Electoral College is a good idea. After all, there have been five presidential elections where the candidate who won the popular vote did not become president. Why? Because of the Electoral College. This happened most recently in 2016. The other dates were 1824, 1876, 1888, and 2000.

Another criticism of the Electoral College is that there is no guarantee the electors will vote for the candidate they pledged to. Others think the winner-takes-all system of electoral votes is unfair. If a presidential candidate gets one more popular vote than his opponent, they can win all of a state's electoral votes.

| Election Year | Number of Faithless Electors |
|---|---|
| 1796 | 19 |
| 1808 | 6 |
| 1812 | 4 |
| 1820 | 1 |
| 1828 | 7 |
| 1832 | 32 |
| 1836 | 23 |
| 1872 | 63 |
| 1892 | 1 |
| 1896 | 27 |
| 1912 | 8 |
| 1848 | 1 |
| 1956 | 1 |
| 1960 | 1 |
| 1968 | 1 |
| 1972 | 1 |
| 1976 | 1 |
| 1988 | 1 |
| 2000 | 1 |
| 2004 | 1 |
| 2016 | 7 |
| TOTAL: 21 elections | 207 |

This chart shows the number of faithless electors from 1796 to 2016. In 21 elections, there were only 207 faithless electors.

## SUPPORTERS OF THE ELECTORAL COLLEGE SYSTEM

But many Americans believe the Electoral College is a great idea. Alexander Hamilton, the country's first secretary of the treasury, was definitely a fan. He said, "I venture somewhat further, and hesitate not to affirm that if the manner of it [the Electoral College] be not perfect, it is at least excellent."

Alexander Hamilton supported the Electoral College's indirect election of the president and vice president.

# Reforming the College

People have proposed changing or getting rid of the Electoral College many times for more than two centuries. In fact, there have been more proposals for constitutional amendments to change the Electoral College than on any other subject! How many? Over 700! But since the Electoral College is part of our Constitution, this can only happen by a constitutional amendment.

In December 2016 there was a campaign to try to convince the Electoral College to vote against President-elect Donald Trump. But the protest was not successful.

# GLOSSARY

**amendment** — a change in the wording or meaning of a document, especially the U.S. Constitution

**ballot** — a process of voting in writing, usually in secret

**delegate** — a person sent to represent others, especially as an elected representative at a conference

**elector** — a member of the Electoral College

**Framer** — one of the delegates who drafted the U.S. Constitution

**majority** — a percentage or number greater than half of the total

**nominate** — propose a candidate for election or for an award or honor

**poll** — place where voters go to cast their vote in an election

**popular vote** — the votes cast by qualified voters among the general population

**prosecute** — to carry on legal proceedings against someone to prove their guilt

**ratify** — to sign or give formal consent to a contract, treaty, or agreement, making it officially valid

**slate** — a list of candidates for election to an office or post, usually made of a group who share similar political views

# FURTHER INFORMATION

## BOOKS

Connors, Kathleen. *What Is the Electoral College?* New York: Gareth Stevens Publishing, 2017.

Ross, Tara. *We Elect a President: The Story of Our Electoral College.* Dallas: Colonial Press L.P., 2016.

Sobel, Syl. *Presidential Elections and Other Cool Facts.* Hauppage, NY: Barron's Educational Series, Inc., 2016.

## ONLINE

PowerKids Press has developed an online list of websites related to the subject of this book. This site is updated regularly. Please use this link to access the list:

**www.powerkidslinks.com/wuwyg/electoral**

**Publisher's note to educators and parents:** Our editors have carefully reviewed these websites to ensure that they are suitable for students. Many websites change frequently, however, and we cannot guarantee that a site's future contents will continue to meet our high standards of quality and educational value. Be advised that students should be closely supervised whenever they access the Internet.

# INDEX


Adams, John Quincy, 14
amendments, 13, 15, 29
ballot, 12, 20, 21, 22
Burr, Aaron, 12, 14
Bush, George W., 22
Certificate of Vote, 25
Clay, Henry, 14
Clinton, Bill, 19
Clinton, Hillary, 7, 23, 27
Congress, 5, 7, 11, 15, 25
Constitution, 10, 11, 12, 13, 17, 26, 29
Crawford, William, 14
Cuomo, Andrew, 19
de Blasio, Bill, 19
Democratic Party, 8, 15, 19, 23
early voting, 21
election date, 5, 20, 21
electors, 6, 8, 11, 12, 13, 16, 17, 18, 19, 20, 21, 23, 25, 26, 27, 28
faithless electors, 26, 27, 28
Faith Spotted Eagle, 27
Founding Fathers, 10, 11, 12
Framers (of Constitution), 10, 11
Gore, Al, 22
Hamilton, Alexander, 29
Hayes, Rutherford B., 15
House of Representatives, 7, 8, 12, 14, 17
inauguration, 20, 24
Ingram, Hazel, 17
Jackson, Andrew, 14
Jefferson, Thomas, 12, 14
Johnson, Richard Mentor, 15
majority, 12, 13, 14
nomination, 18, 19
polls, 4, 5, 9, 20, 22
popular vote, 7, 14, 15, 18, 22, 23, 26, 28
Powell, Colin, 27
Republican Party, 8, 15, 23
Sanders, Bernie, 27
Senate, 7, 15
Tilden, Samuel J., 15
Trump, Donald, 4, 7, 23, 27, 29
Van Buren, Martin, 15
voting, 4, 5, 7, 8, 9, 11, 12, 13, 14, 15, 18, 20, 21, 22, 23, 24, 25, 26, 27, 28